Cyber Crimes

History of World's Worst Cyber Attacks

Vannesa Pitts

Alpha Editions

ISBN : 9789386101709

Design and Setting By
Alpha Editions
(A Vij Publishing Group Company)
www.vijbooks.com
email - contact@vijpublishing.com

Contents

What is Cyber Crime   1

History of Cybercrime   5

Hackers to Cyber-Terrorists   9

World's Most Famous Cyber Crimes & Attacks

MafiaBoy   18

PlayStation Network Outage   23

Sven Jaschan   30

The Spamhaus Project   32

Citigroup Attack   35

Heartland Payment Systems   37

Titan Rain   39

Operation Aurora   42

Opi Israel   51

Stuxnet attack on Iran   55

Project Chanology   60

Canadian government hackings   77

July 2009 cyber attacks   80

OPM Data Breach   83

References   87

Introduction

Computer crime refers to criminal activity involving a computer. The computer may be used in the commission of a crime or it may be the target. Net-crime refers to criminal use of the Internet. Cyber-crimes are essentially a combination of these two elements and can be best defined as "Offences that are committed against individuals or groups of individuals with a criminal motive to intentionally harm the reputation of the victim or cause physical or mental harm to the victim directly or indirectly using modern telecommunication networks such as the Internet (Chat rooms, emails, notice boards and groups) and mobile phones (SMS/MMS)".

In its most simple form, cyber-crime can be defined as any illegal activity that uses a computer as its primary means of function. The U.S. Department of Justice broadens this definition to include any illegal activity that uses a computer for the storage of evidence. The term 'cyber-crime' can refer to offenses including criminal activity against data, infringement of content and copyright, fraud, unauthorized access, child pornography and cyber-stalking.

The United Nations Manual on the Prevention and Control of Computer Related Crime includes fraud, forgery and unauthorized access in its definition of cyber-crime. Cyber-crime in effect covers a wide range of attacks on individuals and organisations alike. These crimes may include anything from an individual's emotional or financial state to a nation's security.

There are two main categories that define the make up of cyber-crimes. Firstly those that target computer networks or devices such as viruses, malware, or denial of service attacks. The second category relate to crimes that are facilitated by computer networks or devices like cyber-stalking, fraud, identity-theft, extortion, phishing (spam) and theft of classified information.

In order to highlight the scale of cyber-crime globally, the Norton Cyber-crime Report 2011 revealed 431 million adults in 24 countries had been victims' of cyber-crime in that year. Computer based crime is escalating at an alarming rate. In the report Norton calculated the financial cost of global cyber-crime at $388 billion. This is more than the combined international market for marijuana, heroin and cocaine, estimated at $288 billion. Assuming its current growth rate continues, cyber-crime will soon surpass the entire global drug trafficking market that is estimated to be worth $411 billion annually.

Cyber-crimes have expanded to include activities that cross international borders and can now be considered a global epidemic. The international legal system ensures cyber criminals are held accountable through the International Criminal Court. Law enforcement agencies are faced with unique challenges and the anonymity of the Internet only complicates the issues. There are problems with gathering evidence, cross-jurisdictional issues and miscommunication related to reporting.

It is widely known that victims of Internet crimes are often reluctant to report an offence to authorities. In some cases the individual or organization may not even be aware a crime has been committed. Even though facilities for reporting incidents of cyber-crime have improved in recent years many victims remain reluctant due essentially to embarrassment.

International cooperation is essential if an effective response is to be found against global cyber-crime. No nation can expect to effectively combat the issue alone. Many computer based crimes are initiated 'off-shore' and this presents enormous challenges to any nations law enforcement agencies. It is critical that agencies from around the world formulate actionable plans to detect, follow, arrest and prosecute cyber criminals.

For example, in the past two years Australia has adopted the National Criminal Intelligence Fusion Capability, a key element of the Commonwealth Organized Crime Strategic Framework (COCSF). This body brings together expertise, data and technology across a range of government and law enforcement agencies and enables international collaboration.

The problem of cyber-crime seems almost immeasurable in size. Looking at recent trends and advances in mobile technology and cloud computing we realize it is an ever-evolving and rapidly changing dynamic. There is growing evidence globally of newly formed partnerships between government and industry aimed at prevention. These partnerships create opportunities to share information and bolster law enforcement response to organized Internet-based crime.

This sharing of information creates concerns in its self. It is an extremely complex and sensitive issue. A balance must be found in efficiently maximizing distribution of information and protecting it from the organized cyber-criminal element.

Cyber-crime covers such a broad scope of criminal enterprise. The examples mentioned above are only a few of the thousands of variants of illegal activities commonly classed as cyber-crimes. Computers and the Internet have improved our lives in many ways, unfortunately criminals now make use of these technologies to the detriment of society.

x

What is Cyber Crime

Computer crime, or cybercrime, is crime that involves a computer and a network. The computer may have been used in the commission of a crime, or it may be the target. Such crimes may threaten a nation's security and financial health. Issues surrounding these types of crimes have become high-profile, particularly those surrounding hacking, copyright infringement, child pornography, and child grooming. There are also problems of privacy when confidential information is intercepted or disclosed, lawfully or otherwise. Internationally, both governmental and non-state actors engage in cybercrimes, including espionage, financial theft, and other cross-border crimes. Activity crossing international borders and involving the interests of at least one nation state is sometimes referred to as cyberwarfare. The international legal system is attempting to hold actors accountable for their actions through the International Criminal Court.

Today, definitions for cybercrime cross over multiple spectra. The following information is a collaboration of definitions built to answer your questions about this growing threat to individuals and organizations. Many of the cyber crime articles available on the Internet today can appear outdated as they fall short of a uniform categorization or specific steps on methods for fighting cybercrime or even how to support cyber crime victims. These barriers also create difficulty for those attempting to report cybercrime. With today's rapid growth of technology, as well as updates to cyber law cannot stop cyber crime from growing and updating in kind. Internet fraud is certainly the area that most personal computer (PC) users are concerned about, and cyber crime study, continues to be left to amateurs or veteran criminologists. It is critical today that both users and organizations comprehend and teach what is cyber crime and how to stop it. The broad meaning of cybercrime can be narrowed down by looking at specific crimes that are most common.

Cyber Identity Theft and Computer Hacking, considered by experts as the most common forms of cybercrime, involve the theft of personal information that is attainable through computer systems and computer networks. Phishing and pharming seem to have the most success as potential victims of these crimes do not think twice when sites that veil their criminal intent, or even look identical to sites familiar to Internet users, which makes it easy for cyber criminals to collect critical online identity information like Full Name, Phone Number, Address, Login, Password, Credit Card/Bank Account numbers

Cyberspace crime involves much more than Identity Theft, and, today, does not even require Internet use. The growth of interest in topics such as cyberbullying, commonly perpetrated through the use of cell phones, is on pace to achieve Identity Theft's level of notoriety. Current Wiki Leak and Hactivist news items have also shown the Global nature of cybercrime, while broadening the cyber crime definition. Protection from these and other cyberspace crimes are quickly becoming popular subjects.

Types of Cyber Crimes

When any crime is committed over the Internet it is referred to as a cyber crime. There are many types of cyber crimes and the most common ones are explained below:

Hacking: This is a type of crime wherein a person's computer is broken into so that his personal or sensitive information can be accessed. In the United States, hacking is classified as a felony and punishable as such. This is different from ethical hacking, which many organizations use to check their Internet security protection. In hacking, the criminal uses a variety of software to enter a person's computer and the person may not be aware that his computer is being accessed from a remote location.

Theft: This crime occurs when a person violates copyrights and downloads music, movies, games and software. There are even peer sharing websites which encourage software piracy and many of these websites are now being targeted by the FBI. Today, the justice system is addressing this cyber crime and there are laws that prevent people from illegal downloading.

Cyber Stalking: This is a kind of online harassment wherein the victim is subjected to a barrage of online messages and emails. Typically, these stalkers know their victims and instead of resorting to offline stalking, they use the Internet to stalk. However, if they notice that cyber stalking is not having the desired effect, they begin offline stalking along with cyber stalking to make the victims' lives more miserable.

Identity Theft: This has become a major problem with people using the Internet for cash transactions and banking services. In this cyber crime, a criminal accesses data about a person's bank account, credit cards, Social Security, debit card and other sensitive information to siphon money or to buy things online in the victim's name. It can result in major financial losses for the victim and even spoil the victim's credit history.

Malicious Software: These are Internet-based software or programs that are used to disrupt a network. The software is used to gain access to a system to steal sensitive information or data or causing damage to software present in the system.

Child soliciting and Abuse: This is also a type of cyber crime wherein criminals solicit minors via chat rooms for the purpose of child pornography. The FBI has been spending a lot of time monitoring chat rooms frequented by children with the hopes of reducing and preventing child abuse and soliciting.

History of Cybercrime

Our modern society demands a degree of connectivity between citizens, businesses, financial institutions and governments that must cross political and cultural boundaries. Digital technology provides this connectivity and gives its users many valuable benefits. But at the same time, it provides a rich environment for criminal activity, ranging from vandalism to stolen identity to theft of classified government information.

Hacking is a term used to describe the activity of modifying a product or procedure to alter its normal function, or to fix a problem. The term purportedly originated in the 1960s, when it was used to describe the activities of certain MIT model train enthusiasts who modified the operation of their model trains. They discovered ways to change certain functions without re-engineering the entire device.

These curious individuals went on to work with early computer systems where they applied their curiosity and resourcefulness to learning and changing the computer code that was used in early programs. Some of their hacks became so successful they outlived the original product, such as the UNIX operating system, developed as a hack by Dennis Ritchie and Keith Thompson of Bell Labs. To the general public a "hack" became known as a clever way to fix a problem with a product, or an easy way to improve its function.

The malicious association with hacking became evident in the 1970s when early computerized phone systems became a target. Technologically savvy individuals, called "phreakers" discovered the correct codes and tones that would result in free long distance service. They impersonated operators, dug through Bell Telephone company garbage to find secret information, and performed countless experiments on early telephone hardware in order to learn how to exploit the system. They were hackers in every sense of the word, using their resourcefulness to modify hardware and software to steal long distance telephone time.

This innovative type of crime was a difficult issue for law enforcement, due in part to lack of legislation to aid in criminal prosecution, and a shortage of investigators skilled in the technology that was being hacked. It was clear that computer systems were open to criminal activity, and as more complex communications became available to the consumer, more opportunities for cyber crime developed.

In 1986 the systems administrator at the Lawrence Berkeley National Laboratory, Clifford Stoll, noted certain irregularities in accounting data. Inventing the first digital forensic techniques, he determined that an unauthorized user was hacking into his computer network. Stoll used what is called a "honey pot tactic," which lures a hacker back into a network until enough data can be collected to track the intrusion to its source. Stoll's effort paid off with the eventual arrest of Markus Hess and a number of others located in West Germany, who were stealing and selling military information, passwords and other data to the KGB.

The Berkeley lab intrusion was soon followed by the discovery of the Morris worm virus, created by Robert Morris, a Cornell University student. This worm damaged more than 6,000 computers and resulted in estimated damages of $98 million. More incidents began to follow in a continuous, steady stream. Congress responded by passing its first hacking-related legislation, the Federal Computer Fraud and Abuse Act, in 1986. The act made computer tampering a felony crime punishable by significant jail time and monetary fines.

In 1990, during a project dubbed Operation Sundevil, FBI agents confiscated 42 computers and over 20,000 floppy disks that were allegedly being used by criminals for illegal credit card use and telephone services. This two-year effort involved 150 agents. Despite the low number of indictments, the operation was seen as a successful public relations effort by law enforcement officials. Garry M. Jenkins, the Assistant Director of the U.S. Secret Service, explained at a press conference that this activity sent a message to criminals that, "they were on the watch everywhere, even in those sleazy and secretive dens of cybernetic vice, the underground boards."

While largely effective, the decisions and activities of law enforcement with regard to investigating cyber crime are not always perfect. If law enforcement makes a mistake, law abiding citizens might suffer. The Steve Jackson Games publishing company was nearly forced out of business after being accused of possessing an illegally copied document. The Secret Service believed this document was in Jackson's possession, and confiscated the computers used in his business. When the equipment was not returned in a timely manner, he was forced to lay off employees, miss deadlines and his business was nearly ruined. When the computers were returned, Jackson discovered that company emails had been accessed and customer data was deleted. The Secret Service never pressed charges for any crime.

The Electronic Frontier Foundation (EFF) formed in 1990 as a response to threats on civil liberties that can occur through overzealous activities and mistakes made by law enforcement personnel who are investigating cyber crime and related matters. It is a collection of technologists, lawyers and other professionals who act to defend and protect consumers from unlawful prosecution.

Crime and cyber crime will continue to be present in our society, regardless of the best efforts of the criminal justice system. The public and private sector need highly skilled individuals to combat this threat and help prevent the prosecution of innocent people. Talented individuals who want to pursue a cybersecurity career in criminal justice must have proficiency with communication technology, understand regulatory concerns and be familiar with homeland security law. Cybersecurity is an exciting field for people with a curious nature and who never tire of learning new things while balancing complex social and technological concerns.

Hackers to Cyber-Terrorists

Professional hackers, either working on their own or employed by the government or military service, can find computer systems with vulnerabilities lacking the appropriate security software. Once found, they can infect systems with malicious code and then remotely control the system or computer by sending commands to view content or to disrupt other computers. There needs to be a pre-existing system flaw within the computer such as no antivirus protection or faulty system configuration for the viral code to work. Many professional hackers will promote themselves to cyberterrorists where a new set of rules govern their actions. Cyberterrorists have premeditated plans and their attacks are not born of rage. They need to develop their plans step-by-step and acquire the appropriate software to carry out an attack. They usually have political agendas, targeting political structures. Cyber terrorists are hackers with a political motivation, their attacks can impact political structure through this corruption and destruction. They also target civilians, civilian interests and civilian installations. As previously stated cyberterrorists attack persons or property and cause enough harm to generate fear.

Types

In detail, there are a number of techniques to utilize in

cyber-attacks and a variety of ways to administer them to individuals or establishments on a broader scale. Attacks are broken down into two categories, Syntactic attacks and Semantic attacks. Syntactic attacks are straight forward; it is considered malicious software which includes viruses, worms, and Trojan horses.

Viruses are a self-replicating program that can attach itself to another program or file in order to reproduce. The virus can hide in unlikely locations in the memory of a computer system and attach itself to whatever file it sees fit to execute its code. It can also change its digital footprint each time it reproduces making it even harder to track down in the computer.

Worms do not need another file or program to copy itself; it is a self-sustaining running program. Worms replicate over a network using protocols. The latest incarnation of worms make use of known vulnerabilities in systems to penetrate, execute their code, and replicate to other systems such as the Code Red II worm that infected more than 259 000 systems in less than 14 hours. On a much larger scale, worms can be designed for industrial espionage to monitor and collect server and traffic activities then transmit it back to its creator.

A Trojan horse is designed to perform legitimate tasks but it also performs unknown and unwanted activity. It can be the basis of many viruses and worms installing onto the computer as keyboard loggers and backdoor software. In a commercial sense, Trojans can be imbedded in trial versions of software and can gather additional intelligence about the target without the person even knowing it happening. All three of these are likely to attack an individual and establishment through emails, web browsers, chat clients, remote software, and updates.

Semantic attack is the modification and dissemination of correct and incorrect information. Information modified could have been done without the use of computers even though new opportunities can be found by using them. To set someone into the wrong direction or to cover your tracks, the dissemination of incorrect information can be utilized.

Once a cyber-attack has been initiated, there are certain targets that need to be attacked to cripple the opponent. Certain infrastructures as targets have been highlighted as critical infrastructures in time of conflict that can severely cripple a nation. Control systems, energy resources, finance, telecommunications, transportation, and water facilities are seen as critical infrastructure targets during conflict. A new report on the industrial cybersecurity problems, produced by the British Columbia Institute of Technology, and the PA Consulting Group, using data from as far back as 1981, reportedly has found a 10-fold increase in the number of successful cyber-attacks on infrastructure Supervisory Control and Data Acquisition (SCADA) systems since 2000. Cyber-attacks that have an adverse physical effect are known as cyber-physical attacks.

Control Systems

Control systems are responsible for activating and monitoring industrial or mechanical controls. Many devices are integrated with computer platforms to control valves and gates to certain physical infrastructures. Control systems are usually designed as remote telemetry devices that link to other physical devices through internet access or modems. Little security can be offered when dealing with these devices, enabling many hackers or cyberterrorists to seek out systematic vulnerabilities. Paul Blomgren, manager of sales engineering at cybersecurity firm explained how his people drove to a remote substation, saw a wireless network antenna and immediately plugged in their wireless LAN cards. They took out their laptops and connected to the system because it wasn't using passwords. "Within 10 minutes, they had mapped every piece of equipment in the facility," Blomgren said. "Within 15 minutes, they mapped every piece of equipment in the operational control network. Within 20 minutes, they were talking to the business network and had pulled off several business reports. They never even left the vehicle."

Energy

Energy is seen as the second infrastructure that could be attacked. It is broken down into two categories, electricity and natural gas. Electricity also known as electric grids power cities, regions, and households; it powers machines and other mechanisms used in day-to-day life. Using U.S. as an example, in a conflict cyberterrorists can access data through the Daily Report of System Status that shows power flows throughout the system and can pinpoint the busiest sections of the grid. By shutting those grids down, they can cause mass hysteria, backlog, and confusion; also being able to locate critical areas of operation to further attacks in a more direct method. Cyberterrorists can access instructions on how to connect to the Bonneville Power Administration which helps direct them on how to not fault the system in the process. This is a major advantage that can be utilized when cyber-attacks are being made because foreign attackers with no prior knowledge of the system can attack with the highest accuracy without drawbacks. Cyber-attacks on natural gas installations go much the same way as it would with attacks on electrical grids. Cyberterrorists can shutdown these installations stopping the flow or they can even reroute gas flows to another section that can be occupied by one of their allies. There was a case in Russia with a gas supplier known as Gazprom, they lost control of their central switchboard which routes gas flow, after an inside operator and Trojan horse program bypassed security.

Finance

Financial infrastructures could be hit hard by cyber-attacks. There is constant money being exchanged in these institutions and if cyberterrorists were to attack and if transactions were rerouted and large amounts of money stolen, financial industries would collapse and civilians would be without jobs and security. Operations would stall from region to region causing nationwide economical degradation. In the U.S. alone, the average daily volume of transactions hit $3 trillion and 99% of it is non-cash flow. To be able to disrupt that amount of money for one day or for a period of days can cause lasting damage making investors pull out of funding and erode public confidence.

Telecommunications

Cyber-attacking telecommunication infrastructures have straightforward results. Telecommunication integration is becoming common practice, systems such as voice and IP networks are merging. Everything is being run through the internet because the speeds and storage capabilities are endless. Denial-of-service attacks can be administered as previously mentioned, but more complex attacks can be made on BGP routing protocols or DNS infrastructures. It is less likely that an attack would target or compromise the traditional telephony network of SS7 switches, or an attempted attack on physical devices such as microwave stations or satellite facilities. The ability would still be there to shut down those physical facilities to disrupt telephony networks. The whole idea on these cyber-attacks is to cut people off from one another, to disrupt communication, and by doing so, to impede critical information being sent and received. In cyberwarfare, this is a critical way of gaining the upper-hand in a conflict. By controlling the flow of information and communication, a nation can plan more accurate strikes and enact better counter-attack measures on their enemies.

Transportation

Transportation infrastructure mirrors telecommunication facilities; by impeding transportation for individuals in a city or region, the economy will slightly degrade over time. Successful cyber-attacks can impact scheduling and accessibility, creating a disruption in the economic chain. Carrying methods will be impacted, making it hard for cargo to be sent from one place to another. In January 2003 during the "slammer" virus, Continental Airlines was forced to shut down flights due to computer problems. Cyberterrorists can target railroads by disrupting switches, target flight software to impede airplanes, and target road usage to impede more conventional transportation methods. In May 2015, a man, Chris Roberts, who was a cyberconsultant, revealed to the FBI that he had repeatedly, from 2011 to 2014, managed to hack into Boeing and Airbus flights' controls via the onboard entertainment system, allegedly, and had at least once ordered a flight to climb. The FBI, after detaining him in April 2015 in Syracuse, had interviewed him about the allegations.

Water

Water as an infrastructure could be one of the most critical infrastructures to be attacked. It is seen as one of the greatest security hazards among all of the computer-controlled systems. There is the potential to have massive amounts of water unleashed into an area which could be unprotected causing loss of life and property damage. It is not even water supplies that could be attacked; sewer systems can be compromised too. There was no calculation given to the cost of damages, but the estimated cost to replace critical water systems could be in the hundreds of billions of dollars. Most of these water infrastructures are well developed making it hard for cyber-attacks to cause any significant damage, at most, equipment failure can occur causing power outlets to be disrupted for a short time.

World's Most Famous
Cyber Crimes & Attacks

MafiaBoy

MafiaBoy was the Internet alias of Michael Calce (born 1986), a high school student from West Island, Quebec, who launched a series of highly publicized denial-of-service attacks in February 2000 against large commercial websites, including Yahoo!, Fifa.com, Amazon.com, Dell, Inc., E*TRADE, eBay, and CNN. He also launched a series of failed simultaneous attacks against 9 of the 13 root name servers. Calce was born in the West Island area of Montreal, Quebec. When he was five, his parents separated and he lived with his mother after she had won a lengthy battle for primary custody. Every second weekend he would stay at his father's condo in Montreal proper. He felt isolated from his friends back home and troubled by the separation of his parents, so his father purchased him his own computer at the age of six. It instantly had a hold on him: "I can remember sitting and listening to it beep, gurgle and churn as it processed commands. I remember how the screen lit up in front of my face. There was something intoxicating about the idea of dictating everything the computer did, down to the smallest of functions. The computer gave me, a six-year-old, a sense of control and command. Nothing else in my world operated that way."

Denial-of-service attack

In computing, a denial-of-service (DoS) attack is an attempt to make a machine or network resource unavailable to its intended users, such as to temporarily or indefinitely interrupt or suspend services of a host connected to the Internet. A distributed denial-of-service (DDoS) is where the attack source is more than one, often thousands of, unique IP addresses. It is analogous to a group of people crowding the entry door or gate to a shop or business, and not letting legitimate parties enter into the shop or business, disrupting normal operations.

Criminal perpetrators of DoS attacks often target sites or services hosted on high-profile web servers such as banks, credit card payment gateways; but motives of revenge, blackmail or activism can be behind other attacks.

The United States Computer Emergency Readiness Team (US-CERT) defines symptoms of denial-of-service attacks to include:

• Unusually slow network performance (opening files or accessing web sites)

• Unavailability of a particular web site

• Inability to access any web site

• Dramatic increase in the number of spam emails received—(this type of DoS attack is considered an e-mail bomb)

- Disconnection of a wireless or wired internet connection

- Long term denial of access to the web or any internet services

If the attack is conducted on a sufficiently large scale, entire geographical regions of Internet connectivity can be compromised without the attacker's knowledge or intent by incorrectly configured or flimsy network infrastructure equipment.

The Attack

On February 7, 2000, Calce targeted Yahoo! with a project he named Rivolta, meaning "riot" in Italian. Rivolta was a denial-of-service attack in which servers become overloaded with different types of communications to the point where they shut down completely. At the time, Yahoo! was a multibillion-dollar web company and the top search engine. Mafiaboy's Rivolta managed to shut down Yahoo! for almost an hour. Calce's goal was, according to him, to establish dominance for himself and TNT, his cybergroup, in the cyberworld. Buy.com was shut down in response. Calce responded to this in turn by bringing down eBay, CNN, Amazon and Dell.com via DDoS over the next week.

In a 2011 interview, Calce tried to redeem his image by saying that the attacks had been launched unwittingly, after inputting known addresses in a security tool he had downloaded from a repository on the now defunct file-sharing platform

Hotline, developed by Hotline Communications. Calce would then have left for school, forgetting the application which continued the attacks during most of the day. Upon coming home Calce found his computer crashed, and restarted it unaware of what had gone on during the day. Calce claimed when he overheard the news and recognized the companies mentioned being those he had inputted earlier in the day, that he "started to understand what might have happened".

The U.S. Federal Bureau of Investigation and the Royal Canadian Mounted Police first noticed Calce when he started claiming in IRC chatrooms that he was responsible for the attacks. He became the chief suspect when he claimed to have brought down Dell's website, an attack that had not been publicized at that time. Information on the source of the attacks was initially discovered and reported to the press by Michael Lyle, chief technology officer of Recourse Technologies. Calce initially denied responsibility but later pled guilty to most of the charges brought against him. His lawyer insisted the child had only run unsupervised tests to help design an improved firewall, whereas trial records indicated the youth showed no remorse and had expressed a desire to move to Italy for its lax computer crime laws. The Montreal Youth Court sentenced him on September 12, 2001 to eight months of "open custody," one year of probation, restricted use of the Internet, and a small fine.

Matthew Kovar, a senior analyst at the market research firm Yankee Group, generated some publicity when he told reporters the attacks caused US$1.2 billion in global economic damages. Media outlets would later attribute a then-1.45:1

conversion value of CAD $1.7 billion to the Royal Canadian Mounted Police. Computer security experts now often cite the larger figure , but a published report says the trial prosecutor gave the court a figure of roughly $7.5 million.

While testifying at a congressional hearing in Washington, D.C., computer expert Winn Schwartau said that "Government and commercial computer systems are so poorly protected today they can essentially be considered defenseless - an Electronic Pearl Harbor waiting to happen." Whether it be banking, business or social networking, most people have various amounts of personal information online. Mafiaboy was the first to demonstrate how accessible this information is to the public and how easily it could be retrieved. The fact that the largest website in the world could be shut down by a 15-year-old created widespread panic. By this time, the internet had already become an integral part of the North American economy. Consumers lost confidence in online business and the American economy suffered a minor blow as a result. Former CIA agent Craig Guent credits Mafiaboy for the significant increase in online security that took place over the decade.

During the latter half of 2005, he wrote a column on computer security topics for Le Journal de Montréal. In late 2008, with journalist Craig Silverman, Calce announced he was writing a book, Mafiaboy: How I Cracked the Internet and Why It's Still Broken.

PlayStation Network Outage

In 2011, 77 millions of Playstation Network and Sony Online Entertainment accounts, including credit and debit card information users were stolen by an unknown group of cyber hackers.PlayStation Network outage was the result of an "external intrusion" on Sony's PlayStation Network and Qriocity services, in which personal details from approximately 77 million accounts were compromised and prevented users of PlayStation 3 and PlayStation Portable consoles from accessing the service. The attack occurred between April 17 and April 19, 2011, forcing Sony to turn off the PlayStation Network on April 20.

On May 4 Sony confirmed that personally identifiable information from each of the 77 million accounts had been exposed. The outage lasted 23 days. At the time of the outage, with a count of 77 million registered PlayStation Network accounts, it was one of the largest data security breaches in history. It surpassed the 2007 TJX hack which affected 45 million customers. Government officials in various countries voiced concern over the theft and Sony's one-week delay before warning its users.

Sony stated on April 26 that it was attempting to get online services running "within a week." On May 14, Sony released PlayStation 3 firmware version 3.61 as a security patch. The firmware required users to change their password upon signing in. At the time the firmware was released, the network was still offline. Regional restoration was announced by Kazuo Hirai, CEO of Sony Corporation. A map of regional restoration and the network within the United States was shared as the service was coming back online.

The Attack

On April 20, 2011, Sony acknowledged that on the official PlayStation Blog that it was "aware certain functions of the PlayStation Network" were down. Upon attempting to sign in via the PlayStation 3, users received a message indicating that the network was "undergoing maintenance". The following day, Sony asked its customers for patience while the cause of outage was investigated and stated that it may take "a full day or two" to get the service fully functional again.

The company later announced an "external intrusion" had affected the PlayStation Network and Qriocity services. This intrusion occurred between April 17 and April 19. On April 20, Sony suspended all PlayStation Network and Qriocity services worldwide. Sony expressed their regrets for the downtime and called the task of repairing the system "time-consuming" but would lead to a stronger network infrastructure and additional security. On April 25, Sony spokesman Patrick Seybold reiterated on the PlayStation Blog that fixing and enhancing the network was a "time intensive" process with no estimated time of completion. However, the next day Sony stated that there was a "clear path to have PlayStation Network and Qriocity systems back online", with some services expected to be restored within a week. Furthermore, Sony acknowledged the "compromise of personal information as a result of an illegal intrusion on our systems."

On May 1 Sony announced a "Welcome Back" program for customers affected by the outage. The company also confirmed that some PSN and Qriocity services would be available during the first week of May. The list of services expected to become available included:

- Restoration of Online game-play across the PlayStation 3 (PS3) and PSP (PlayStation Portable) systems

- This includes titles requiring online verification and downloaded games

- Access to Music Unlimited powered by Qriocity for PS3/PSP for existing subscribers

- Access to account management and password reset

- Access to download un-expired Movie Rentals on PS3, PSP and MediaGo

- PlayStation Home

- Friends List

- Chat Functionality

On May 2 Sony issued a press release, according to which the Sony Online Entertainment (SOE) services had been taken offline for maintenance due to potentially related activities during the initial criminal hack. Over 12,000 credit card numbers, albeit in encrypted form, from non-U.S. cardholders and additional information from 24.7 million SOE accounts may have been accessed.

During the week, Sony sent a letter to the US House of Representatives, answering questions and concerns about the event. In the letter Sony announced that they would be providing Identity Theft insurance policies in the amount of $1 million USD per user of the PlayStation Network and Qriocity services, despite no reports of credit card fraud being indicated. This was later confirmed on the PlayStation Blog, where it was announced that the service, AllClear ID Plus powered by Debix, would be available to users in the United States free for 12 months, and would include Internet surveillance, complete identity repair in the event of theft and a $1 million identity theft insurance policy for each user.

On May 6 Sony stated they had begun "final stages of internal testing" for the PlayStation Network, which had been rebuilt. However, the following day Sony reported that they would not be able to bring services back online within the one-week timeframe given on May 1, because "the extent of the attack on Sony Online Entertainment servers" had not been known at the time. SOE confirmed on their Twitter account that their games would not be available until sometime after the weekend.

Reuters began reporting the event as "the biggest Internet security break-in ever". A Sony spokesperson said:

• Sony had removed the personal details of 2,500 people stolen by hackers and posted on a website

• The data included names and some addresses, which were in a database created in 2001

• No date had been fixed for the restart

On May 14 various services began coming back online on a country-by-country basis, starting with North America. These services included: sign-in for PSN and Qriocity services (including password resetting), online game-play on PS3 and PSP, playback of rental video content, Music Unlimited service (PS3 and PC), access to third party services (such as Netflix, Hulu, Vudu and MLB.tv), friends list, chat functionality and PlayStation Home. The actions came with a firmware update for the PS3, version 3.61. As of May 15 service in Japan and East Asia had not yet been approved.

On May 18 SOE shut down the password reset page on their site following the discovery of another exploit that allowed users to reset other users' passwords, using the other user's email address and date of birth. Sign-in using PSN details to various other Sony websites was also disabled, but console sign-ins were not affected.

On May 23 Sony stated that the outage costs were $171 million.

World Government Reactions

The data theft concerned authorities around the world. Graham Cluley, senior technology consultant at Sophos, said the breach "certainly ranks as one of the biggest data losses ever to affect individuals".

The British Information Commissioner's Office stated that Sony would be questioned, and that an investigation would take place to discover whether Sony had taken adequate precautions to protect customer details. Under the UK's Data Protection Act, Sony was fined £250,000 for the breach.

Privacy Commissioner of Canada Jennifer Stoddart confirmed that the Canadian authorities would investigate. The Commissioner's office conveyed their concern as to why the authorities in Canada weren't informed of a security breach earlier.

US Senator Richard Blumenthal of Connecticut demanded answers from Sony about the data breach by emailing SECA CEO Jack Tretton arguing about the delay in informing its customers and insisting that Sony do more for its customers than just offer free credit reporting services. Blumenthal later called for an investigation by the US Department of Justice to find the person or persons responsible and to determine if Sony was liable for the way that it handled the situation.

Congresswoman Mary Bono Mack and Congressman G. K. Butterfield sent a letter to Sony, demanding information on when the breach was discovered and how the crisis would be handled.

Sony had been asked to testify before a congressional hearing on security and to answer questions about the breach of security on May 2, but sent a written response instead.

Legal action against Sony

A lawsuit was posted on April 27 by Kristopher Johns from Birmingham, Alabama on behalf of all PlayStation users alleging Sony "failed to encrypt data and establish adequate firewalls to handle a server intrusion contingency, failed to provide prompt and adequate warnings of security breaches, and unreasonably delayed in bringing the PSN service back online." According to the complaint filed in the lawsuit, Sony failed to notify members of a possible security breach and storing members' credit card information, a violation of PCI Compliance—the digital security standard for the Payment Card Industry.

A Canadian lawsuit against Sony USA, Sony Canada and Sony Japan claimed damages up to C$1 billion including free credit monitoring and identity theft insurance. The plaintiff was quoted as saying, "If you can't trust a huge multi-national corporation like Sony to protect your private information, who can you trust? It appears to me that Sony focuses more on protecting its games than its PlayStation users".

In October 2012 a Californian judge dismissed a lawsuit against Sony over the PSN security breach, ruling that Sony had not violated Californian consumer-protection laws, citing "there is no such thing as perfect security".

In 2013 United Kingdom Information Commissioner's Office charged Sony with a £250,000 penalty for putting a large amount of personal and financial data of PSN clients at risk.

Sven Jaschan

Sven Jaschan a German college student who confessed as the author of Netsky worms and Sasser computer worms, had unleashed a virus in 2004 on his 18th birthday that has resounding effects all around the world. Though the estimated damage was pegged at $500 million dollars, experts believed that it could have been more as it disabled the Delta Air Lines' computer system and resulted in a number of cancellations of several transatlantic flights. Microsoft placed a $250,000 bounty on his head. He was captured after a three-month manhunt operation.

Jaschan lived in the village of Waffensen, Germany, and attended a computer science school in nearby Rotenburg. He was a shy & quiet person, possibly diagnosed with autism/asperger syndrome. He admitted writing and releasing the two damaging worms when arrested by German police on 7 May 2004 after a three-month-long international investigation. Following his arrest, Microsoft confirmed that they had received tip-offs from more than one source, and that the $250,000 reward for identifying the author of the NetSky worm would be shared between them. A Microsoft official attended the arrest and the initial interrogation. Some sources claim that at least one tip-off came from a classmate of Jaschan's to whom he had boasted of his activities. Several of Jaschan's classmates also came under investigation following Jaschan's arrest. There was also speculation that he had written the worms to drum up business for his mother and stepfather's PC support business and was actively working on an antidote to the worm. In an interview in July 2004, Jaschan claimed to have written the Netsky worms in order to remove infection with Mydoom and Bagle worms from victims' computers.

He also confirmed that a classmate had given a tip to Microsoft. A report by Sophos in August 2004 claimed that Jaschan's viruses were responsible for 70% of the infections seen in the first half of that year. Following his initial arrest, Jaschan was released pending trial. Several companies and institutions have posted damage claims against him. According to the Rotenburg-Wuemme State Court, four German lawsuits were settled for under $1,000 each.

Jaschan was tried as a minor because the German courts determined that he created the virus before he was 18. The virus was released on his 18th birthday (April 29, 2004). Sven Jaschan was found guilty of computer sabotage and illegally altering data. On Friday, July 8, 2005, he received a 21-month suspended sentence. He later received three years probation and had to complete 30 hours of community service in a retirement home.

The Spamhaus Project

Considered as the biggest cyber attack in history, Spamhaus, a filtering service used to weed out spam emails, was subjected to cyber attacks wherein home and business broadband router owners became unsuspecting participants when their routers have been threatened. Thousands of Britons used Spamhaus on a daily basis determine whether or not to accept incoming mails. On March 18, 2013, Spamhaus added Cyberbunker to its blacklisted sites and Cyberbunker and other hosting companies retaliated by hiring hackers to put up botnets, which also exploited home and broadband routers, to shut down Spamhaus' system.

CyberBunker dispute and DDoS attack

In March 2013, CyberBunker, an internet provider named after its former headquarters in a surplus NATO bunker in the Netherlands that "offers anonymous hosting of anything except child porn and anything related to terrorism" was added to the Spamhaus blacklist used by email providers to weed out spam. Shortly afterwards, beginning on March 18, Spamhaus was the target of a distributed denial of service (DDoS) attack exploiting a long-known vulnerability in the Domain Name System (DNS) which permits origination of massive quantities of messages at devices owned by others using IP address spoofing. Devices exploited in the attack may be as simple as a cable converter box connected to the internet. The attack was of a previously unreported scale (peaking at 300 gigabits per second; an average large-scale attack might reach 50 Gbit/s, and the largest previous publicly reported attack was 100 Gbit/s) was launched against Spamhaus's DNS servers; as of 27 March 2013 the effects of the attack had lasted for over a week. Steve Linford, chief executive for Spamhaus, said that they had withstood the attack, using the assistance of other internet companies such as Google to absorb the excess traffic. Linford also claimed that the attack was being investigated by five different national cyber-police-forces around the world, who had chosen to remain anonymous to avoid similar attacks on their own infrastructure. Spamhaus also hired Cloudflare, a DDoS mitigation company, to assist them by distributing their internet services across Cloudflare's worldwide network, after which the focus of the attack was redirected to the companies that provide Cloudflare's network connections.

Spamhaus alleged that CyberBunker, in cooperation with "criminal gangs" from Eastern Europe and Russia, was behind the attack; CyberBunker did not respond to the BBC's request for comment on the allegation, however Sven Olaf Kamphuis, the owner of CyberBunker, posted to his Facebook account on 23 March "Yo anons, we could use a little help in shutting down illegal slander and blackmail censorship project 'spamhaus.org,' which thinks it can dictate its views on what should and should not be on the Internet." According to The New York Times Kamphuis also claimed to be the spokesman of the attackers, and said in a message "We are aware that this is one of the largest DDoS attacks the world had publicly seen", and that CyberBunker was retaliating against Spamhaus for "abusing their influence". The NYT added that security researcher Dan Kaminsky said "You can't stop a DNS flood ... The only way to deal with this problem is to find the people doing it and arrest them".

The attack was attributed by network engineers to an anonymous group unhappy with Spamhaus, later identified by the victims of the attack as Stophaus, a loosely organized group of "bulletproof spam and malware hosters".

On 26 April 2013 the owner of CyberBunker, Sven Olaf Kamphuis, was arrested in Spain for his part in the attack on Spamhaus. He has since been released pending trial.

The British National Cyber Crime Unit revealed that a London schoolboy had been secretly arrested as part of a suspected organised crime gang responsible for the DDoS attacks. The newspaper quotes a briefing document on the British investigation, codenamed Operation Rashlike, about the arrest:

> "The suspect was found with his computer systems open and logged on to various virtual systems and forums. The subject has a significant amount of money flowing through his bank account. Financial investigators are in the process of restraining monies."

The boy's arrest, by detectives from the National Cyber Crime Unit, followed an international police operation against those suspected of carrying out the massive cyber attack, which slowed down the internet worldwide.

Citigroup Attack

Citigroup, one of the largest financial giants in the world, provides an ample incentive for hackers to organize an attack due to the vast amount of wealth and sensitive information that flows through the company daily. In 2011, over 200,000 customer information from contact details to account numbers were compromised, which resulted in $2.7 million loss for the company.

Citigroup said that the attck affected almost twice as many accounts as the bank's figures had initially suggested, as major U.S. lenders come under growing pressure from lawmakers to improve account security. A total of 360,083 North American Citigroup credit card accounts were affected by the breach. Of those affected, some 217,657 customers were reissued with new cards along with a notification letter, while the remaining accounts were either inactive or had already received new cards earlier.

Customers had their names, account numbers and contact information accessed, but Citi said that "data critical to commit fraud was not compromised" and that other consumer banking online systems were not accessed.

In the Citi breach, the data thieves were able to penetrate the bank's defenses by first logging on to the site reserved for its credit card customers. The method is seemingly simple, but the fact that the thieves knew to focus on this particular vulnerability marks the Citigroup attack as especially ingenious, security experts said.

Once inside, they leapfrogged between the accounts of different Citi customers by inserting vari-ous account numbers into a string of text located in the browser's address bar. The hackers' code systems automatically repeated this exercise tens of thousands of times — allowing them to capture the confidential private data.

On June 13, 2011 The New York Times website had an article which read "Thieves Found Citigroup Site an Easy Entry", Think of it as a mansion with a high-tech security system — but the front door wasn't locked tight.

Heartland Payment Systems

The trusted payment processor Heartland Payment Systems also fell into the trap set by Albert Gonzales of the Shadowcrew fame, which were responsible for phishing out over 100 million individual card numbers, costing Heartland more then $140 million dollars in damages incurred in 2008. Besides the damages incurred, it also besmirched the company's motto, "The highest standards – The Most Trusted Transactions."

Heartland Payment Systems suffered a data breach on May 8th that affected their payroll customers. This is unfortunate news when you take into account that they analysts were of a mind that the company would be posting a $0.64 earnings per share. The payroll processing company also has product offerings in loyalty cards, mobile payments and payment processing. Heartland paid out roughly $140 million in fines and other penalties as a result. In the end, a single person went to jail.

While the company continues to assess the damages inflicted by the attack, Robert Baldwin, the company's president and CFO, says law enforcement has already noted that the attack against his company is part of a wider cyber fraud operation. Heartland, headquartered in Princeton, NJ, handles approximately 100 million transactions per month, although the number of unique cardholders is much lower. It is still a question as to the percentage of the data flow they were able to get.

Titan Rain

Titan Rain was the designation given by the federal government of the United States to a series of coordinated attacks on American computer systems since 2003; they were known to have been ongoing for at least three years. The attacks were labeled as Chinese in origin, although their precise nature, e.g., state-sponsored espionage, corporate espionage, or random hacker attacks, and their real identities – masked by proxy, zombie computer, spyware/virus infected – remain unknown. The activity known as "Titan Rain" is believed to be associated with an Advanced Persistent Threat.

In early December 2005 the director of the SANS Institute, a security institute in the United States, said that the attacks were "most likely the result of Chinese military hackers attempting to gather information on U.S. systems."

Titan Rain hackers gained access to many United States defense contractor computer networks who were targeted for their sensitive information, including those at Lockheed Martin, Sandia National Laboratories, Redstone Arsenal, and NASA. The series of attacks are believed by some to be the actions of the People's Liberation Army (PLA), rather than some freelance Chinese hackers. These hackers attacked both the American (Defense Intelligence Agency – DOD) and British Government Departments (Ministry of Defence – MOD). The British government had an incident in 2006 where a part of the House of Commons computer system was shut down by - initially thought to be an individual – an "organised Chinese hacking group." Although most of the evidence has pointed to the Chinese government as the attackers, China have claimed that it was not them who attacked the United States, leading to another possibility that it was hackers using Chinese computers.

'Titan Rain' has caused friction between the U.S. and Chinese governments as, although with little evidence, the U.S. government has blamed the Chinese government for the attacks of 2004 on the unclassified, although potentially fatal information. Adam Paller, SANS Institute research director, stated that the attacks came from individuals with "intense discipline," and that, "no other organisation could do this if they were not a military". Such sophistication and evidence has pointed toward the Chinese military (People's Liberation Army) as the attackers.

'Titan Rain' reportedly attacked multiple high-end political systems, such as NASA and the FBI. Although no sensitive and classified information was reported stolen, the hackers were however able to steal unclassified information (e.g. information from a home computer). The fact that the information was classified or not was somewhat irrelevant; when it all comes together it could reveal the strengths and weaknesses of the U.S., making such an attack very damaging. 'Titan Rain' has caused distrust between other countries (such as the United Kingdom and Russia – other superpowers) and China. Such distrust has occurred because these countries were likely attacked, but either did not detect an attack or have not released statements that they were attacked. The United Kingdom have stated officially that their governmental offices were attacked by hackers of a Chinese source. The events of 'Titan Rain' have caused the rest of the world to be more cautious of attacks; not just from China, but from other countries as well, thereby causing, however small, a slight distrust between other countries. This distrust between them may affect future agreements and dealings and as such further affect their relationship with China.

Operation Aurora

Operation Aurora was a series of cyber attacks conducted by advanced persistent threats such as the Elderwood Group based in Beijing, China, with ties to the People's Liberation Army. First publicly disclosed by Google on January 12, 2010, in a blog post, the attacks began in mid-2009 and continued through December 2009.

The attack has been aimed at dozens of other organizations, of which Adobe Systems, Juniper Networks and Rackspace have publicly confirmed that they were targeted. According to media reports, Yahoo, Symantec, Northrop Grumman, Morgan Stanley and Dow Chemical were also among the targets.

As a result of the attack, Google stated in its blog that it plans to operate a completely uncensored version of its search engine in China "within the law, if at all", and acknowledged that if this is not possible it may leave China and close its Chinese offices. Official Chinese sources claimed this was part of a strategy developed by the U.S. government.

The attack was named "Operation Aurora" by Dmitri Alperovitch, Vice President of Threat Research at cyber security company McAfee. Research by McAfee Labs discovered that "Aurora" was part of the file path on the attacker's machine that was included in two of the malware binaries McAfee said were associated with the attack. "We believe the name was the internal name the attacker(s) gave to this operation," McAfee Chief Technology Officer George Kurtz said in a blog post.

According to McAfee, the primary goal of the attack was to gain access to and potentially modify source code repositories at these high tech, security and defense contractor companies. "The SCMs were wide open," says Alperovitch. "No one ever thought about securing them, yet these were the crown jewels of most of these companies in many ways — much more valuable than any financial or personally identifiable data that they may have and spend so much time and effort protecting."

On January 12, 2010, Google revealed on its blog that it had been the victim of a cyber attack. The company said the attack occurred in mid-December and originated from China. Google stated that over 20 other companies had been attacked; other sources have since cited that more than 34 organizations were targeted. As a result of the attack, Google said it was reviewing its business in China. On the same day, United States Secretary of State Hillary Clinton issued a brief statement condemning the attacks and requesting a response from China.

On January 13, 2010, the news agency All Headline News reported that the United States Congress plans to investigate Google's allegations that the Chinese government used the company's service to spy on human rights activists.

In Beijing, visitors left flowers outside of Google's office. However, these were later removed, with a Chinese security guard stating that this was an "illegal flower tribute". The Chinese government has yet to issue a formal response, although an anonymous official stated that China is seeking more information on Google's intentions.

Technical evidence including IP addresses, domain names, malware signatures, and other factors, show Elderwood was behind the Operation Aurora attack, one of numerous attacks conducted by the Elderwood gang and others such as PLA Unit 61398, a Shanghai-based advanced persistent threat group also called "Comment Crew", named after the technique often used by the group involving internal software "comment" features on web pages, which are used to infiltrate target computers that access the sites. The two largest groups may employ hundreds of people, and work to compromise security and siphon business ideas, advanced designs, and trade secrets from various foreign computer networks. The group behind the Operation Aurora attacks were dubbed "Elderwood" by Symantec after a source-code variable used by the attackers, and "Beijing Group" by Dell Secureworks. The group obtained some of Google's source code, as well as access to information about Chinese activists. Along with other groups such as Unit 61398, also targeted numerous other companies in the shipping, aeronautics, arms, energy, manufacturing, engineering, electronics, financial, and software sectors.

Elderwood specializes in attacking and infiltrating second-tier defense industry suppliers that make electronic or mechanical components for top defense companies. Those firms then become a cyber "stepping stone" to gain access to top-tier defense contractors. One attack procedure used by

Elderwood is to infect legitimate websites frequented by employees of the target company – a so-called "water hole" attack, just as lions stake out a watering hole for their prey. Elderwood infects these less-secure sites with malware that downloads to a computer that clicks on the site. After that, the group searches inside the network to which the infected computer is connected, finding and then downloading executives' e-mails and critical documents on company plans, decisions, acquisitions, and product designs.

In its blog posting, Google stated that some of its intellectual property had been stolen. It suggested that the attackers were interested in accessing Gmail accounts of Chinese dissidents. According to the Financial Times, two accounts used by Ai Weiwei had been attacked, their contents read and copied; his bank accounts were investigated by state security agents who claimed he was under investigation for "unspecified suspected crimes". However, the attackers were only able to view details on two accounts and those details were limited to things such as the subject line and the accounts' creation date.

Security experts immediately noted the sophistication of the attack. Two days after the attack became public, McAfee reported that the attackers had exploited purported zero-day vulnerabilities (unfixed and previously unknown to the target system developers) in Internet Explorer and dubbed the attack "Operation Aurora". A week after the report by McAfee, Microsoft issued a fix for the issue, and admitted that they had known about the security hole used since September. Additional vulnerabilities were found in Perforce, the source code revision software used by Google to manage their source code. VeriSign's iDefense Labs claimed that the attacks were perpetrated by "agents of the Chinese state or proxies thereof".

According to a diplomatic cable from the U.S. Embassy in Beijing, a Chinese source reported that the Chinese Politburo directed the intrusion into Google's computer systems. The cable suggested that the attack was part of a coordinated campaign executed by "government operatives, public security experts and Internet outlaws recruited by the Chinese government." The report suggested that it was part of an ongoing campaign in which attackers have "broken into American government computers and those of Western allies, the Dalai Lama and American businesses since 2002." According to The Guardian's reporting on the leak, the attacks were "orchestrated by a senior member of the Politburo who typed his own name into the global version of the search engine and found articles criticising him personally."

Once a victim's system was compromised, a backdoor connection that masqueraded as an SSL connection made connections to command and control servers running in Illinois, Texas, and Taiwan, including machines that were running under stolen Rackspace customer accounts. The victim's machine then began exploring the protected corporate intranet that it was a part of, searching for other vulnerable systems as well as sources of intellectual property, specifically the contents of source code repositories.

The attacks were thought to have definitively ended on Jan 4 when the command and control servers were taken down, although it is not known at this point whether or not the attackers intentionally shut them down. However, the attacks were still occurring as of February 2010.

The German, Australian, and French governments publicly issued warnings to users of Internet Explorer after the attack, advising them to use alternative browsers at least until a fix for the security hole was made. The German, Australian, and French governments consider all versions of Internet Explorer vulnerable or potentially vulnerable.

In an advisory on January 14, 2010, Microsoft said that attackers targeting Google and other U.S. companies used software that exploits a hole in Internet Explorer. The vulnerability affects Internet Explorer versions 6, 7, and 8 on Windows 7, Vista, Windows XP, Server 2003, Server 2008 R2, as well as IE 6 Service Pack 1 on Windows 2000 Service Pack 4.

The Internet Explorer exploit code used in the attack has been released into the public domain, and has been incorporated into the Metasploit Framework penetration testing tool. A copy of the exploit was uploaded to Wepawet, a service for detecting and analyzing web-based malware operated by the computer security group at the University of California, Santa Barbara. "The public release of the exploit code increases the possibility of widespread attacks using the Internet Explorer vulnerability," said George Kurtz, CTO of McAfee, of the attack. "The now public computer code may help cyber criminals craft attacks that use the vulnerability to compromise Windows systems."

Security company Websense said it identified "limited public use" of the unpatched IE vulnerability in drive-by attacks against users who strayed onto malicious Web sites. According to Websense, the attack code it spotted is the same as the exploit that went public last week. "Internet Explorer users currently face a real and present danger due to the public disclosure of the vulnerability and release of attack code, increasing the possibility of widespread attacks," said George Kurtz, chief technology officer of McAfee, in a blog update. Confirming this speculation, Websense Security Labs identified additional sites using the exploit on January 19. According to reports from Ahnlab, the second URL was spread through the Instant Messenger network Misslee Messenger, a popular IM client in South Korea.

Researchers have created attack code that exploits the vulnerability in Internet Explorer 7 (IE7) and IE8—even when Microsoft's recommended defensive measure (Data Execution Prevention (DEP)) is turned on. According to Dino Dai Zovi, a security vulnerability researcher, "even the newest IE8 isn't safe from attack if it's running on Windows XP Service Pack 2 (SP2) or earlier, or on Windows Vista RTM (release to manufacturing), the version Microsoft shipped in January 2007."

Microsoft admitted that the security hole used had been known to them since September. Work on an update was prioritized and on Thursday, January 21, 2010, Microsoft released a security patch aiming to counter this weakness, the published exploits based on it and a number of other privately reported vulnerabilities. They did not state if any of the latter had been used or published by exploiters or whether these had any particular relation to the Aurora operation, but the entire cumulative update was termed critical for most versions of Windows, including Windows 7.

Security researchers have continued to investigate the attacks. HBGary, a security firm, recently released a report in which they claim to have found some significant markers that might help identify the code developer. The firm also said that the code was Chinese language based but could not be specifically tied to any government entity.

On February 19, 2010, a security expert investigating the cyber-attack on Google, has claimed that the people behind the attack were also responsible for the cyber-attacks made on several Fortune 100 companies in the past one and a half years. They have also tracked the attack back to its point of origin, which seems to be two Chinese schools, Shanghai Jiao Tong University and Lanxiang Vocational School. As highlighted by The New York Times, both of these schools have ties with the Chinese search engine Baidu, a rival of Google China. Both Lanxiang Vocational and Jiaotong University have denied the allegation.

In March 2010, Symantec, which was helping investigate the attack for Google, identified Shaoxing as the source of 21.3% of all (12 billion) malicious emails sent throughout the world.

To prevent future cyberattacks such as Operation Aurora, Amitai Etzioni of the Institute for Communitarian Policy Studies has suggested that China and the United States agree to a policy of mutually assured restraint with respect to cyberspace. This would involve allowing both states to take the measures they deem necessary for their self-defense while simultaneously agreeing to refrain from taking offensive steps; it would also entail vetting these commitments.

Opi Israel

A coordinated cyber attack by anti-Israel groups and individuals, #opiIsrael is a DDoS assault that was timed for April 7, 2012, the eve of Holocaust Remembrance Day with the aim of erasing Israel from the internet. Websites targeted by these hactivists include financial and business sectors, educational institutions, non-profit organizations, newspapers, and privately-owned businesses in Israel. Anonymous took down a bunch of Israeli government websites on Sunday and say they caused over $3 billion in damage. But they didn't totally get away with it. Within a few hours of the attack which Anonymous says affected 100,000 websites, 40,000 Facebook pages, 5,000 Twitter accounts and 30,000 bank accounts, an Israeli hacker broke into the website that Anonymous had set up for the attack, dubbed Operation Israel. Instead of the original anti-Israel messages that were originally on the site to protest Israel's treatment of Palestine, the Israeli hacker rejiggered the site to play "Hatikvah," Israel's national anthem.

In the leadup to the attack, Israeli organizations made preparations to defend their websites, and cyber-security experts called on home users to increase awareness and take precautions such as changing passwords, not opening strange or suspicious emails, and maintaining especial vigilance when using Facebook. The Israel Internet Association (ISOC) operated a hotline for people to report attacks and published real-time status reports on its website.

Ultimately, #OpIsrael caused no physical damage and was assessed by the Israeli Government's National Cyber Bureau and by some security experts and journalists to have been a failure.

Target

Larger than Life, an Israeli NGO devoted to "improving the quality of life and welfare of cancer-stricken children and their families regardless of sex, religion and nationality", stated that in the week leading up to #OpIsrael, its website was targeted repeatedly by pro-Palestinian hackers who defaced it with "flags, a skull, symbols, and all sorts of hate-related things".

Yad Vashem, Israel's national Holocaust museum, came under a "fairly massive attack". Nevertheless, its website was fully operational on the day of the attack, which overlapped with Holocaust Remembrance Day.

At midday, #OpIsrael activists announced on Twitter that they had defaced the website of an Israeli hair salon, Peter Hair, in Ramat HaSharon. The salon's home page showed a masked person holding a sign saying "Indonesian Security Down #OP ISRAHELL" and was signed with the message "We are Muslims, Soldier of Allah". The owner of the salon, Peter Imseis, said he had not been aware that the site had been hacked and that it had not affected his business.

Government websites that experienced problems on 7 April 2013 included those of the Israeli Ministry of Education and Central Bureau of Statistics, but it was unclear whether these problems were caused by #OpIsrael.

During the day, attackers posted numerous claims of successes, such as "Anonymous causes Israel to lose $5 billion" in stock market losses and "Tel Aviv loses all Internet connection".

The attack was praised by Hamas, the militant Islamist group that controls the Gaza Strip. Hamas spokesman Ihab al-Ghussain wrote: "May God protect the spirit and mission of the soldiers of this electronic war". A statement on the website of the Tunisian Renaissance Party, signed by party leader Rashid Al-Ghannouchi, expressed "condemnation of all those who do not pursue a policy of dialogue to reach its objectives and follow the methods of terrorists to reach its goals", and threatening "to prosecute anyone involved from Tunisia in attacks on Israel on charges of compromising the security of a foreign state". Tunisians quickly mobilized against the party, with some lawyers offering to defend hackers charged with attacking Israel free of charge. The Renaissance Party later issued a different statement saying that their website had itself been hacked and that the party does not condemn cyberattacks on Israel.

The attack drew a response by pro-Israel hackers, who quickly took over #OpIsrael's official website OpIsrael.com and filled it with pro-Israel content. The DNS record of opisrael.com showed a purchase made under the name 'Al Qaeda'. OpIsrael claimed after the site was hacked that it had never been their official website. Israeli Elite Force had an early start forming two days prior to the attack, taking down Iranian, Pakistani, Turkish government website and leaking information on Twitter. They received coverage in the world media.

Stuxnet attack on Iran

Iran was subjected to cyber attacks on June 2010 when its nuclear facility in Natanz was infected by Stuxnet, a cyber worm that was believed to be a combined effort of Israel and the United States, though no one claimed responsibility for its inception. The worm destroyed Tehran's 1000 nuclear centrifuges and set back the country's atomic program by at least two years, as it spread beyond the plant and infected over 60,000 computers as well. The Iranian government was also accused of its own cyber attacks to the United States, Israel and other countries in the Gulf Arabs, including their alleged involvement in the hacking of American banks in 2012.

Origin of Stuxnet

Stuxnet is a malicious computer worm believed to be a jointly built American-Israeli cyber weapon. Although neither state has confirmed this openly, anonymous US officials speaking to the Washington Post claimed the worm was developed during the Obama administration to sabotage Iran's nuclear program with what would seem like a long series of unfortunate accidents.

Stuxnet specifically targets PLCs, which allow the automation of electromechanical processes such as those used to control machinery on factory assembly lines, amusement rides, or centrifuges for separating nuclear material. Exploiting four zero-day flaws, Stuxnet functions by targeting machines using the Microsoft Windows operating system and networks, then seeking out Siemens Step7 software. Stuxnet reportedly compromised Iranian PLCs, collecting information on industrial systems and causing the fast-spinning centrifuges to tear themselves apart. Stuxnet's design and architecture are not domain-specific and it could be tailored as a platform for attacking modern SCADA and PLC systems (e.g., in automobile or power plants), the majority of which reside in Europe, Japan and the US. Stuxnet reportedly ruined almost one-fifth of Iran's nuclear centrifuges.

Stuxnet has three modules: a worm that executes all routines related to the main payload of the attack; a link file that automatically executes the propagated copies of the worm; and a rootkit component responsible for hiding all malicious files and processes, preventing detection of the presence of Stuxnet.

Stuxnet is typically introduced to the target environment via an infected USB flash drive. The worm then propagates across the network, scanning for Siemens Step7 software on computers controlling a PLC. In the absence of either criterion, Stuxnet becomes dormant inside the computer. If both the conditions are fulfilled, Stuxnet introduces the infected rootkit onto the PLC and Step7 software, modifying the codes and giving unexpected commands to the PLC while returning a loop of normal operations system values feedback to the users.

In 2015, Kaspersky Labs' research findings on another highly sophisticated espionage platform created by what they called the Equation Group, noted that the group had used two of the same zero-day attacks used by Stuxnet, before they were used in Stuxnet, and their use in both programs was similar. The researchers reported that "the similar type of usage of both exploits together in different computer worms, at around the same time, indicates that the EQUATION group and the Stuxnet developers are either the same or working closely together".

Experts believe that Stuxnet required the largest and costliest development effort in malware history. Developing its many capabilities would have required a team of highly capable programmers, in-depth knowledge of industrial processes, and an interest in attacking industrial infrastructure. The Guardian, the BBC and The New York Times all claimed that (unnamed) experts studying Stuxnet believe the complexity of the code indicates that only a nation-state would have the capabilities to produce it.

On 23 November 2010 it was announced that uranium enrichment at Natanz had ceased several times because of a series of major technical problems. A "serious nuclear accident" (supposedly the shutdown of some of its centrifuges) occurred at the site in the first half of 2009, which is speculated to have forced the head of Iran's Atomic Energy Organization Gholam Reza Aghazadeh to resign. Statistics published by the Federation of American Scientists (FAS) show that the number of enrichment centrifuges operational in Iran mysteriously declined from about 4,700 to about 3,900 beginning around the time the nuclear incident WikiLeaks mentioned would have occurred. The Institute for Science and International Security (ISIS) suggests, in a report published in December 2010, that Stuxnet is "a reasonable explanation for the apparent damage" at Natanz, and may have destroyed up to 1000 centrifuges (10 percent) sometime between November 2009 and late January 2010.

The ISIS report further notes that Iranian authorities have attempted to conceal the breakdown by installing new centrifuges on a large scale.

The worm worked by first causing an infected Iranian IR-1 centrifuge to increase from its normal operating speed of 1,064 hertz to 1,410 hertz for 15 minutes before returning to its normal frequency. Twenty-seven days later, the worm went back into action, slowing the infected centrifuges down to a few hundred hertz for a full 50 minutes. The stresses from the excessive, then slower, speeds caused the aluminum centrifugal tubes to expand, often forcing parts of the centrifuges into sufficient contact with each other to destroy the machine.

According to The Washington Post, IAEA cameras installed in the Natanz facility recorded the sudden dismantling and removal of approximately 900–1000 centrifuges during the time the Stuxnet worm was reportedly active at the plant. Iranian technicians, however, were able to quickly replace the centrifuges and the report concluded that uranium enrichment was likely only briefly disrupted.

The head of the Bushehr Nuclear Power Plant told Reuters that only the personal computers of staff at the plant had been infected by Stuxnet and the state-run newspaper Iran Daily quoted Reza Taghipour, Iran's telecommunications minister, as saying that it had not caused "serious damage to government systems". The Director of Information Technology Council at the Iranian Ministry of Industries and Mines, Mahmud Liaii, has said that: "An electronic war has been launched against Iran... This computer worm is designed to transfer data about production lines from our industrial plants to locations outside Iran."

In response to the infection, Iran has assembled a team to combat it. With more than 30,000 IP addresses affected in Iran, an official has said that the infection is fast spreading in Iran and the problem has been compounded by the ability of Stuxnet to mutate. Iran has set up its own systems to clean up infections and has advised against using the Siemens SCADA antivirus since it is suspected that the antivirus is actually embedded with codes which update Stuxnet instead of eradicating it.

Project Chanology

Project Chanology was a protest movement against the practices of the Church of Scientology by members of Anonymous, a leaderless Internet-based group that defines itself as ubiquitous. The project was started in response to the Church of Scientology's attempts to remove material from a highly publicized interview with Scientologist Tom Cruise from the Internet in January 2008.

The project was publicly launched in the form of a video posted to YouTube, "Message to Scientology", on January 21, 2008. The video states that Anonymous views Scientology's actions as Internet censorship, and asserts the group's intent to "expel the church from the Internet". This was followed by distributed denial-of-service attacks (DDoS), and soon after, black faxes, prank calls, and other measures intended to disrupt the Church of Scientology's operations. In February 2008, the focus of the protest shifted to legal methods, including nonviolent protests and an attempt to get the Internal Revenue Service to investigate the Church of Scientology's tax exempt status in the United States. Reactions from the Church of Scientology regarding the protesters' actions have varied. Initially, one spokesperson stated that members of the group "have got some wrong information" about Scientology. Another referred to the group as a group of "computer geeks".

Later, the Church of Scientology started referring to Anonymous as "cyberterrorists" perpetrating "religious hate crimes" against the church.

Detractors of Scientology have also criticized the actions of Project Chanology, asserting that they merely provide the Church of Scientology with the opportunity to "play the religious persecution card". Other critics such as Mark Bunker and Tory Christman initially questioned the legality of Project Chanology's methods, but have since spoken out in support of the project as it shifted towards nonviolent protests and other legal methods. The Church of Scientology has a history of conflict with groups on the Internet. In 1995, attorneys for the Church of Scientology attempted to get the newsgroup alt.religion.scientology (a.r.s.) removed from Usenet. This attempt backfired and generated a significant amount of press for a.r.s. The conflict with a.r.s led the hacker group Cult of the Dead Cow to declare war on the Church of Scientology. The Church of Scientology mounted a 10-year legal campaign against Dutch writer Karin Spaink and several Internet service providers after Spaink and others posted documents alleged to be secret teachings of the organization. The Church of Scientology's efforts ended in a legal defeat in a Dutch court in 2005. This series of events is often referred to as "Scientology versus the Internet".

The Church of Scientology has a history of conflict with groups on the Internet. In 1995, attorneys for the Church of Scientology attempted to get the newsgroup alt.religion.scientology (a.r.s.) removed from Usenet. This attempt backfired and generated a significant amount of press for a.r.s. The conflict with a.r.s led the hacker group Cult of the Dead Cow to declare war on the Church of Scientology. The Church of Scientology mounted a 10-year legal campaign against Dutch writer Karin Spaink and several Internet service providers after Spaink and others posted documents alleged to be secret teachings of the organization. The Church of Scientology's efforts ended in a legal defeat in a Dutch court in 2005. This series of events is often referred to as "Scientology versus the Internet".

Tom Cruise video

On January 14, 2008, a video produced by the Church of Scientology featuring an interview with Tom Cruise was posted on YouTube. In the video, music from Cruise's Mission: Impossible films plays in the background, and Cruise makes various statements, including saying that Scientologists are the only people who can help after a car accident, and that Scientologists are the authority on getting addicts off drugs. According to The Times, Cruise can be seen in the video "extolling the virtues of Scientology". The Daily Telegraph (Australia) characterized Cruise as "manic-looking" during the interview, "gushing about his love for Scientology".

The Church of Scientology asserted that the video material that had been leaked to YouTube and other websites was "pirated and edited" and taken from a three-hour video produced for members of Scientology. YouTube removed the Cruise video from their site under threat of litigation. The web site Gawker.com did not take down their copy of the Tom Cruise video, and other sites have posted the entire video.

Lawyers for the Church of Scientology sent a letter to Gawker.com requesting the removal of the video, but Nick Denton of Gawker.com stated: "It's newsworthy and we will not be removing it."

Project Chanology was formulated by users of the English-speaking imageboards 711chan.org and 4chan, the associated partyvan.info wiki, and several Internet Relay Chat channels, all part of a group collectively known as Anonymous, on January 16, 2008 after the Church of Scientology issued a copyright violation claim against YouTube for hosting material from the Cruise video. The effort against Scientology has also been referred to by group members as "Operation Chanology". A webpage called "Project Chanology", part of a larger wiki, is maintained by Anonymous and chronicles planned, ongoing and completed actions by project participants. The website includes a list of suggested guerrilla tactics to use against the Church of Scientology. Members use other websites as well to coordinate action, including Encyclopedia Dramatica and the social networking site Facebook, where two groups associated with the movement had 3,500 members as of February 4, 2008. A member of Anonymous told the Los Angeles Times that, as of February 4, 2008, the group consisted of "a loose confederation of about 9,000 people" who post anonymously on the Internet. A security analyst told The Age that the number of people participating anonymously in Project Chanology could number in the thousands: "You can't pin it on a person or a group of people. You've thousands of people engaged to do anything they can against Scientology."

Members of Project Chanology say their main goal is "to

enlighten the Church of Scientology (CoS) by any means necessary." Their website states: "This will be a game of mental warfare. It will require our talkers, not our hackers. It will require our dedicated Anon across the world to do their part." Project Chanology's stated goals include the complete removal of the Church of Scientology's presence from the Internet and to "save people from Scientology by reversing the brainwashing". Project Chanology participants plan to join the Church of Scientology posing as interested members in order to infiltrate the organization. Andrea Seabrook of National Public Radio's All Things Considered reported Anonymous was previously known for "technologically sophisticated pranks" such as spamming chat rooms online and "ordering dozens of pizzas for people they don't like". Ryan Singel of Wired appeared on the program on January 27, 2008, and told Seabrook that members of Anonymous were motivated by "the tactics the Church of Scientology uses to control information about itself" rather than the "controversial nature of Scientology itself".

Internet activities

Project Chanology began its campaign by organizing and delivering a series of denial-of-service attacks against Scientology websites and flooding Scientology centers with prank calls and black faxes. The group was successful in taking down local and global Scientology websites intermittently from January 18, 2008 until at least January 25, 2008. Anonymous had early success rendering major Scientology websites inaccessible and leaking documents allegedly stolen from

Scientology computers. This resulted in a large amount of coverage on social bookmarking websites.

The denial-of-service attacks on Scientology.org flooded the site with 220 megabits of traffic, a mid-range attack. Speaking with SCMagazineUS.com, a security strategist for Top Layer Networks, Ken Pappas said that he thought that botnets were involved in the Anonymous operation: "There are circles out there where you could take ownership of the bot machines that are already owned and launch a simultaneous attack against something like the church from 50,000 PCs, all at the same time".

In response to the attacks, on January 21, 2008 the Scientology.org site was moved to Prolexic Technologies, a company specializing in safeguarding web sites from denial-of-service attacks. Attacks against the site increased, and CNET News reported that "a major assault" took place at 6 p.m. EST on January 24, 2008. Anonymous escalated the attack on Scientology on January 25, 2008 and on January 25, 2008, the Church of Scientology's official website remained inaccessible.

On January 21, 2008, Anonymous announced its goals and intentions via a video posted to YouTube entitled "Message to Scientology", and a press release declaring "War on Scientology", against both the Church of Scientology and the Religious Technology Center. In the press release, the group stated that the attacks against the Church of Scientology would continue in order to protect freedom of speech and to end what they characterized as the financial exploitation of church members.

The Tom Cruise video is referred to specifically at the start of the Anonymous YouTube video posting, and is characterized as a "propaganda video". The video utilizes a synthesized voice and shows floating cloud images using a time lapse method as the speaker addresses the leaders of Scientology directly: "We shall proceed to expel you from the Internet and systematically dismantle the Church of Scientology in its present form..." The video goes on to state: "We recognize you as serious opponents, and do not expect our campaign to be completed in a short time frame. However, you will not prevail forever against the angry masses of the body politic. Your choice of methods, your hypocrisy, and the general artlessness of your organization have sounded its death knell. You have nowhere to hide because we are everywhere... We are Anonymous. We are Legion. We do not forgive. We do not forget. Expect us." By January 25, 2008, only four days after its release, the video had been viewed 800,000 times, and by February 8, 2008 had been viewed over 2 million times. Author Warren Ellis called the video "creepy in and of itself" and a "manifesto, declaration of war, sharp political film".

In a different video posted to YouTube, Anonymous addresses news organizations covering the conflict and criticizes media reporting of the incident. In the video, Anonymous criticizes the media specifically for not mentioning objections by the group to certain controversial aspects of the history of the Church of Scientology, and cited past incidents including the death of Lisa McPherson: "We find it interesting that you did not mention the other objections in your news reporting. The stifling and punishment of dissent within the totalitarian organization of Scientology. The numerous, alleged human rights violations. Such as the treatment and events that led to the deaths of victims of the cult such as Lisa McPherson." Lisa McPherson was a Scientologist who died in 1995 under controversial circumstances. Initially, the Church of Scientology was held responsible and faced felony charges in her death. The charges were later dropped and a civil suit brought by McPherson's family was settled in 2004. This second video was removed on January 25, 2008, YouTube citing a "terms of use violation". Organizers of the February 10, 2008, Project Chanology protests against the Church of Scientology told the St. Petersburg Times the event was timed to coincide with the birthday of Lisa McPherson.

In addition to DDoS attacks against Church of Scientology websites, Anonymous also organized a campaign on one of their websites to "begin bumping Digg", referring to an attempt to drive up Scientology-related links on the website Digg.com. On January 25, 2008, eight of the top ten stories on Digg.com were about either Scientology-related controversies or Anonymous and attempts to expose Scientology. Digg CEO Jay Adelson told PC World that Anonymous had not manipulated the site's algorithm system to prevent artificial poll results, stating: "They must have done a very good job of bringing in a diverse set of interests ... It just happened to hit a nerve that the Digg community was interested in." Adelson said two other instances which similarly have dominated the Digg main page in the past were the Virginia Tech Massacre in the aftermath of the incident and the "7/7" London bombings in 2005. Adelson commented on the popularity of Scientology theme within the Digg community: "In the history of Digg, there's no question that the topic of Scientology has been of great interest to the community ... I can't explain why."

On January 29, 2008, Jason Lee Miller of WebProNews reported that a Google bomb technique had been used to make the Scientology.org main website the first result in a Google search for "dangerous cult". Miller wrote that Anonymous was behind the Google bomb, and that they had also tried to bump Scientology up as the first result in Google searches for "brainwashing cult", and to make the Xenu.net website first result in searches for "scientology". Rob Garner of MediaPost Publications wrote: "The Church of Scientology continues to be the target of a group called Anonymous, which is using Google bombs and YouTube as its tools of choice."

In a February 4, 2008, article, Scientology spokeswoman Karin Pouw told the Los Angeles Times that Church of Scientology's websites "have been and are online." Danny McPherson, chief research officer at Arbor Networks, claimed 500 denial-of-service attacks had been observed on the Scientology site in the week prior to February 4, some of which were strong enough to bring the website down. Calling Anonymous a "motley crew of internet troublemakers", Wired blogger Ryan Singel said that, while attempting to bypass the Prolexic servers protecting the Church of Scientology website, users of a misconfigured DDoS tool inadvertently and briefly had targeted the Etty Hillesum Lyceum, a Dutch secondary school in Deventer. Another hacking group associated with the project, calling themselves the "g00ns", mistakenly targeted a 59-year-old man from Stockton, California. They posted his home telephone number, address and his wife's Social Security number online for other people to target. They believed that he was behind counter-attacks against Project Chanology-related websites by the Regime, a counter-hack group who crashed one of the Project Chanology planning websites. The group allegedly attempted to gain personal information on people involved in Project Chanology to turn that information over to the Church of Scientology. After discovering they had wrongly targeted the couple, one of the members of the g00ns group called and apologized.

Protests planned

A new video entitled "Call to Action" appeared on YouTube on January 28, 2008, calling for protests outside Church of Scientology centers on February 10, 2008. As with the previous videos, the two-minute video used a synthesized computer voice and featured stock footage of clouds and sky. The video was accompanied by a text transcript with British English spelling. The video denied that the group was composed of "super hackers", stating: "Contrary to the assumptions of the media, Anonymous is not 'a group of super hackers.' ... Anonymous is everyone and everywhere. We have no leaders, no single entity directing us." The video said that Project Chanology participants include "individuals from all walks of life ... united by an awareness that someone must do the right thing." Specific controversies involving the CoS were cited in the video as the explanation for actions by Anonymous.

In an email to CNET News, Anonymous stated that coordinated activities were planned for February 10, 2008, in many major cities around the world. Anonymous hoped to use "real world" protests to rally public opinion to their cause.

According to the Associated Press, the protests were meant to draw attention to what the group refers to as a "vast money-making scheme under the guise of 'religion'". By January 30, 2008, 170 protests had been planned outside Church of Scientology centers worldwide. A video posted to YouTube called "Code of Conduct" outlined twenty-two rules to follow when protesting, and urged protestors to remain peaceful.

Campaign against Scientology's tax-exempt status

A woman who stated she was a member of Anonymous told KNTV that the group has shifted strategy to activities which fight Scientology but are not deemed illegal by the United States government, including an attempt to get the Internal Revenue Service to investigate the Church of Scientology's 501(c)(3) tax-exempt status. Another woman from Anonymous told Newsweek that the group plans to accomplish this through a lobbying campaign. United States tax authorities removed the Church of Scientology's tax-exemption status in 1967, stating that the organization's auditing techniques served as a for-profit operation for L. Ron Hubbard. In 1984, the United States Tax Court ruled that the Church of Scientology was guilty of "manufacturing and falsifying records to present to the IRS, burglarizing IRS offices and stealing government documents, and subverting government processes for unlawful purposes." The Church of Scientology's tax-exempt status in the United States was reinstated in 1993.

A member of Anonymous calling herself "Envie" told Today Tonight that the group has longer term plans against the Church of Scientology: "We are incredibly determined ...

There are those of us who have been talking about plans for the next 12 to 18 months." A member of Anonymous calling herself "Sarah" spoke with Radar magazine about a letter-writing campaign: "We're sending letters to senators and congresspeople requesting that their tax-exempt status be looked at."

Church of Scientology response

In a January 25, 2008 statement made to News.com.au, a spokesman for the Church of Scientology said, "These types of people have got some wrong information about us." A Toronto, Canada spokesperson for the Church of Scientology said she didn't "give a damn" if the group Anonymous was responsible for disrupting access to the Scientology site. Church spokeswoman Yvette Shank told Sun Media that she thought the Anonymous members were a "pathetic" group of "computer geeks". On January 26, 2008, CNET News reported that Karin Pouw, public affairs director for the Church of Scientology, did not address their specific request for a comment about the denial-of-service attacks but instead only responded to the appearance of the Tom Cruise video on YouTube. Pouw stated that the video consisted of "pirated and edited" excerpts of Cruise from a 2004 Scientology event, and that after the video appeared, there was increased traffic to Scientology sites as shown by top lists compiled by search engines. Pouw went on to state "Those wishing to find out the Church of Scientology's views and to gain context of the video have the right to search official Church Web sites if they so desire."

On January 28, 2008, Radar Online reported that the

Church of Scientology asked the U.S. Attorney General's office in Los Angeles, the Federal Bureau of Investigation, and the Los Angeles Police Department to start a criminal investigation of possible criminal activity related to the DDoS attacks. An unnamed source told Radar that the Church of Scientology argued to law enforcement that the Internet attacks are a form of "illegal interference with business." Radar also reported that in statements to law enforcement the Church of Scientology emphasized its status as a religious organization in the United States in order to assert that the DDoS attacks can be classed as hate crimes. The day after the Church of Scientology complained to law enforcement about the DDoS attacks, one of the main Project Chanology sites was down, and a message on the site said that their site crashed due to attacks from Scientologists. In a statement issued to Wikinews, a Church of Scientology employee confirmed that actions of Anonymous had been reported to law enforcement: "Activities of Anonymous have been reported to the Authorities and actions are being taken. Their activities are illegal and we do not approve of them. At the same time, our main work is to improve the environment, make people more able and spiritually aware. ... yes, we are taking action."

The Church of Scientology issued a statement explaining the website move to Prolexic Technologies: "The attacks have defaced and rendered inoperable a number of CoS web sites. But as a very wealthy institution, the Church has fought back with technological answers. On January 21, the Church of Scientology moved its domain to Prolexic Technologies, a group that specializes in protecting Web sites from {denial of service} attacks by creating a safe tunnel by filtering all incoming mail and then allowing only clean messages through."

Lee Sheldon of the Church of Scientology of Orlando and Lee Holzinger of the Church of Scientology of Santa Barbara issued similar statements regarding the February 2, 2008 protests in Florida and California, respectively. Sheldon stated "we recognize the right to legal protest", and Holzinger said "People have the right to express themselves ... The Church of Scientology has always defended the right of freedom of expression." Both representatives also expressed concerns regarding the spread of "hate speech".

The Church of Scientology released a statement regarding the February 10, 2008 worldwide protests, which was published February 7, 2008 in the St. Petersburg Times. In the statement, the Church of Scientology called the organizers of the protests "cyberterrorists", and stated: "We take this seriously because of the nature of the threats this group has made publicly. We will take every step necessary to protect our parishioners and staff as well as members of the community, in coordination with the local authorities." The statement also referred to the actions of members of Project Chanology as "hate crimes" and "religious bigotry", and in a media release said that the group is guided by Communist Manifesto and Mein Kampf; one of the organizers of the protest responded to the latter allegation by stating: "I don't know where they got that from, but I don't think that's true considering that I am a capitalist and a Jew". Pat Harney, spokeswoman for the Church of Scientology in Clearwater, Florida told the St. Petersburg Times: "We are dealing with a worldwide threat ... This is not a light matter." In preparation for the February 10, 2008 protests outside Scientology's spiritual headquarters in Clearwater, the Church of Scientology spent $4,500 to hire ten off-duty police officers for security. Clearwater Police Department spokeswoman Elizabeth Daly-Watts stated that the off-duty police officers will make sure that protesters do not trespass on Scientology property or violate the law, but will report to police supervisors and not representatives of the Church of Scientology.

The Church of Scientology posted a YouTube video claiming that Anonymous are "terrorists" and alleging that Anonymous is perpetrating "hate crimes" against the church. The video does not provide any evidence supporting their claims, and the FBI has not named any suspects for several of the threats mentioned. Anonymous has denied involvement in the more severe accusations. The church also released a DVD containing the YouTube video. The DVD called Anonymous a "dangerous" group and accused them of making threats against Scientology. Men claiming to be from the law firm Latham and Watkins delivered the DVD to family members of at least one person who protested.

YouTube user "AnonymousFacts", which Radar Online described as an associate of Scientology, displayed the names and personal information of several supposed Anonymous members and accused the group of violent threats and terrorism. YouTube quickly took the video down and suspended the "AnonymousFacts" account.

The Church of Scientology sought an injunction and a restraining order to prevent Anonymous from protesting on March 15, 2008, citing threats allegedly made by Anonymous.

Both the injunction and the restraining order were denied. On March 31, 2008, Radar Online reported that representatives of law firms delivered legal letters to suspected Anons, often at their homes. The Church filed complaints of trespassing and criminal harassment against Boston organizer Gregg Housh, who was charged with disturbing an assembly of worship, disturbing the peace, and harassment. The District Attorney's office dropped the harassment charge, and Judge Thomas Horgan issued a continuance without finding for the remaining charges.

In a May 8, 2008 appearance on CNN, Church of Scientology spokesman Thomas W. Davis said that Scientology was "dealing with ninety-six death threats, bomb threats, acts of violence, vandalism" from the group Anonymous. CNN's John Roberts responded, stating that the Federal Bureau of Investigation found nothing connecting Anonymous to the Church of Scientology's accusations of violence: "You are leveling these accusations at this group, the F.B.I., which is looking into it, says it has found nothing to connect this group Anonymous with what you're talking about, or death threats against members of the church, the F.B.I. at this point says - it has no reason to believe that charges would be leveled against this group."

Canadian government hackings

In 2011, news sources revealed that the Government of Canada suffered cyber attacks by foreign hackers using IP addresses from China. The hackers managed to infiltrate three departments within the government and transmit classified information back to them. The attacks resulted in the government cutting off internet access in the departments affected and various responses from both the Canadian government and the Chinese government.

In May 2010 a memo by the Canadian Security Intelligence Service (CSIS) from 2009 was released to the public that warned that cyber attacks on Canadian government, university, and industry computers was showing growth in 2009 and that the threat of cyber attacks was "one of the fastest growing and most complicated issues" facing CSIS. Minister of Public Safety Vic Toews stated in January 2011 that cyber attacks are a serious threat to Canada and that attacks on government computers have grown "quite substantial." In the fall of 2010 the federal government began to strategize ways to prevent cyber attacks and create response plans, which would include $90 million over five years in combating cyber threats.

Auditor General Sheila Fraser has previously warned that the federal government's computer systems risk being breached. In 2002 she stated that the government's internet security was not adequate and warned that it had "weaknesses in the system" and urged improving security to deal with the vulnerabilities. In 2005 she sad the government still has to "translate its policies and standards into consistent, cost-effective practices that will result in a more secure IT environment in departments and agencies."

The cyber attack was first detected in January 2011 and implemented as a phishing scheme. Emails with seemingly innocuous attachments were sent, supposedly by known public servants. The attachments contained malware which infected the computer and exfiltrated key information such as passwords. This information, once sent back to the hackers, could then be used to remotely access the computer and forward the email (with infecting attachment) onto others in order to proliferate the virus.

Affected departments included Treasury Board and the federal Finance Department, as well as a DND agency advising the Canadian armed forces on science and technology. Once detected, Canadian cybersecurity officials shut down all internet access from these departments in order to halt the exfiltration of information from hijacked computers. This left thousands of public servants without internet access.

While the cyber attacks were traced back to Chinese IP addresses, there is "no way of knowing whether the hackers are Chinese, or some other nationality routing their cybercrimes through China to cover their tracks".

When the attacks were detected internet access in the two departments was shut down to prevent stolen information from being sent back to the hackers. The Prime Minister's office have only claimed the hackers made an "attempt to access" servers and did not comment further. A spokesman for Treasury Board Minister Stockwell Day said there were no indications that any data related to Canadians was compromised. CSIS officials have advised the government to not name China as the attacker and not talk about the attacks, while a government official stated Chinese espionage has become a problem for Canada and other countries.

On February 17, Prime Minister Stephen Harper stated that the government has "a strategy in place to try and evolve our systems as those who would attack them become more sophisticated" and that cyber attacks are "a growing issue of importance, not just in this country, but across the world." The same day, Stockwell Day also stated that the attacks weren't " the most aggressive attack but it was a significant one, significant that they were going after financial records."

The Chinese government has denied involvement in the attacks. Foreign Ministry Spokesman Ma Zhaoxu said at a press conference on February 17 that the Chinese government opposes hacking and other criminal acts, saying that "the allegation that China supports hacking is groundless."

July 2009 cyber attacks

The July 2009 cyber attacks were a series of coordinated cyber attacks against major government, news media, and financial websites in South Korea and the United States. The attacks involved the activation of a botnet—a large number of hijacked computers—that maliciously accessed targeted websites with the intention of causing their servers to overload due to the influx of traffic, known as a DDoS attack. Most of the hijacked computers were located in South Korea. The estimated number of the hijacked computers varies widely; around 20,000 according to the South Korean National Intelligence Service, around 50,000 according to Symantec's Security Technology Response group, and more than 166,000 according to a Vietnamese computer security researcher who analyzed the log files of the two servers the attackers controlled. The timing and targeting of the attacks have led to suggestions that they may be from North Korea, although these suggestions have not been substantiated.

Attack

The first wave of attacks occurred on July 4, 2009 (Independence Day holiday in the United States), targeting both the United States and South Korea. Among the websites affected were those of the White House and The Pentagon.

An investigation revealed that 27 websites were targets in the attack based on files stored on compromised systems.

The second wave of attacks occurred on July 7, 2009, affecting South Korea. Among the websites targeted were the presidential Blue House, the Ministry of Defense, the Ministry of Public Administration and Security, the National Intelligence Service and the National Assembly.

A third wave of attacks began on July 9, 2009, targeting several websites in South Korea, including the country's National Intelligence Service as well as one of its largest banks and a major news agency. The U.S. State Department said on July 9 that its website also came under attack. State Department spokesman Ian Kelly said: "I'm just going to speak about our website, the state.gov website. There's not a high volume of attacks. But we're still concerned about it. They are continuing." U.S. Department of Homeland Security spokesperson Amy Kudwa said that the department was aware of the attacks and that it had issued a notice to U.S. federal departments and agencies to take steps to mitigate attacks.

Despite the fact that the attacks have targeted major public and private sector websites, the South Korean Presidential office has suggested that the attacks are targeted towards causing disruption, rather than stealing data. However, Jose Nazario, manager of a U.S. network security firm, claimed that the attack is estimated to have produced only 23 megabits of data per second, not enough to cause major disruptions. Joe Stewart, researcher at SecureWorks' Counter Threat Unit, said that the data generated by the attacking program appeared to be based on a Korean-language browser. It was expected that the economic costs associated with websites being down would be large, as the disruption had prevented people from carrying out transactions, purchasing items or conducting business.

It is not known who is behind the attacks. Reports indicate that the type of attacks being used, commonly known as distributed denial-of-service attacks, were unsophisticated. Given the prolonged nature of the attacks, they are being recognized as a more coordinated and organized series of attacks. According to the South Korean National Intelligence Service, the source of the attacks was tracked down and the government activated an emergency cyber-terror response team who blocked access to five host sites containing the malicious code and 86 websites that downloaded the code, located in 16 countries, including the United States, Guatemala, Japan and the People's Republic of China, but North Korea was not among them. Later, it has been discovered that the malicious code responsible for causing the attack, identified as W32.Dozer, is programmed to destroy data on infected computers and to prevent the computers from being rebooted. South Korean police are analyzing a sample of the thousands of computers used to crash websites, stating that there is "various evidence" of North Korean involvement, but said they may not find the culprit. Security experts said that the attack re-used code from the Mydoom worm. One analyst thinks that the attacks likely came from the United Kingdom. On October 30, 2009, South Korea's spy agency, the National Intelligence Service, stated the origin of the attacks were from North Korea's telecommunications ministry.

OPM Data Breach

In June 2015, the United States Office of Personnel Management (OPM) announced that it had been the target of a data breach targeting the records of as many as four million people. Later, FBI Director James Comey put the number at 18 million. The data breach, which had started in March 2014, and may have started earlier, was noticed by the OPM in April 2015. It has been described by federal officials as among the largest breaches of government data in the history of the United States. Information targeted in the breach included personally identifiable information such as Social Security numbers, as well as names, dates and places of birth, and addresses. The hack went deeper than initially believed and likely involved theft of detailed security-clearance-related background information. One victim wrote that the OPM is the agency that asks your neighbors what they know about you that could be used to blackmail you.

On July 9, 2015, the estimate of the number of stolen records had increased to 21.5 million. This included records of people who had undergone background checks, but who were not necessarily current or former government employees.

The infiltration was discovered using United States Computer Emergency Readiness Team (US-CERT)'s Einstein intrusion-detection program and it predated the Einstein deployment, which began a year earlier. However, the Wall Street Journal, Wired, Ars Technica, and Fortune later reported that it was unclear how the breach was discovered. It may have been a product demonstration of CyFIR, a commercial forensic product from a Manassas, Virginia security company CyTech Services that uncovered the infiltration.

On June 11, 2015, ABC News also said that highly sensitive 127-page Standard Forms (SF) 86 (Questionnaire for National Security Positions) were put at serious risk by the hack. SF-86 forms contain information about family members, college roommates, foreign contacts, and psychological information. At the time, OPM stated that family members names were not compromised. However, on June 13, 2015, OPM spokesman Samuel Schumach said that investigators had "a high degree of confidence that OPM systems containing information related to the background investigations of current, former, and prospective federal government employees, to include U.S. military personnel, and those for whom a federal background investigation was conducted, may have been exfiltrated." The Central Intelligence Agency, however, does not use the OPM system; therefore, it may not have been affected.•

J. David Cox, president of the American Federation of Government Employees, wrote in a letter to OPM director Katherine Archuleta (obtained by the Associated Press) that, based on the incomplete information that the AFGE had received from OPM, "We believe that the Central Personnel Data File was the targeted database, and that the hackers are now in possession of all personnel data for every federal employee, every federal retiree, and up to one million former federal employees." Cox stated that the AFGE believes that the breach compromised military records, veterans' status information, addresses, dates of birth, job and pay history, health insurance and life insurance information, pension information, and data on age, gender, and race. The stolen data included 5.6 million sets of fingerprints. Biometrics expert Ramesh Kesanupalli said that because of this, secret agents were no longer safe, as they could be identified by their fingerprints, even if their names had been changed.

U.S. government officials suspect that Chinese hackers perpetrated the breach. The Washington Post has also reported that the attack originated in China, citing unnamed government officials. China has responded to these claims by noting that it has been the target of cyberattacks in the past. It remains unclear whether the attack, if it originated from China, was sponsored by China's government or not. U.S. Department of Homeland Security official Andy Ozment testified that the attackers had gained valid user credentials to the systems they were attacking, likely through social engineering. The breach also consisted of a malware package which installed itself within OPM's network and established a backdoor. From there, attackers escalated their privileges to gain access to a wide range of OPM's systems. Ars Technica reported that at least one worker with root access to every row in every database was physically located in China. Another contractor had two employees with Chinese passports.

Whether the attack was motivated by commercial gain remains unclear. It has been suggested that hackers working for the Chinese military intend to compile a database of

Americans using the data obtained from the breach.

The OPM had been warned multiple times of security vulnerabilities and failings. A March 2015 OPM Office of the Inspector General semi-annual report to Congress warned of "persistent deficiencies in OPM's information system security program," including "incomplete security authorization packages, weaknesses in testing of information security controls, and inaccurate Plans of Action and Milestones."

A July 2014 story in The New York Times quoted unnamed senior American officials saying that Chinese hackers had broken into OPM. The officials said that the hackers seemed to be targeting files on workers who had applied for security clearances, and had gained access to several databases, but had been stopped before they obtained the security clearance information. In an interview later that month, Katherine Archuleta, the director of OPM, said that the most important thing was that no personal identification information had been compromised.

A July 22, 2015 memo by Inspector General Patrick McFarland said that OPM's Chief Information Officer Donna Seymour was slowing his investigation into the breach, leading him to wonder whether or not she was acting in good faith. He did not raise any specific claims of misconduct, but he did say that her office was fostering an "atmosphere of mistrust" by giving him "incorrect or misleading" information.

References

http://www.floridatechonline.com/resources/cybersecurity-information-assurance/a-brief-history-of-cyber-crime/

http://www.crossdomainsolutions.com/

http://www.crossdomainsolutions.com/cyber-crime/

http://www.wired.com/2009/12/ye_cybercrimes/

http://list25.com/25-biggest-cyber-attacks-in-history/

https://www.theguardian.com/technology/2007/sep/04/news.internet

Graham, Bradley (2005-08-25). "Hackers Attack Via Chinese Web Sites". Washington Post.

Espiner, Tom (2005-11-23). "Security experts lift lid on Chinese hack attacks". ZDNet News. Archived from the original on 2006-12-11.

Thornburgh, Nathan (2005-08-25). "Inside the Chinese Hack Attack". Time.com.

Thornburgh, Nathan (2005-08-29). "The Invasion of the Chinese Cyberspies (And the Man Who Tried to Stop Them)". Time.

Brenner, Bill (2005-08-31). "Myfip's Titan Rain connection". SearchSecurity.com.

Onley, Dawn S.; Wait, Patience (2007-08-21). "Red Storm Rising". Government Computing News.

Norton-Taylor, Richard (2007-09-05). "Titan Rain - how Chinese hackers targeted Whitehall". theguardian.com.

h t t p : / / w w w . t e d . c o m / t a l k s / ralph_langner_cracking_stuxnet_a_21st_century_cyberweapon

Winkler, Ian (2005-10-20). "Guard against Titan Rain hackers". computerworld.com.

Bodmer, Kilger, Carpenter, & Jones (2012). Reverse Deception: Organized Cyber Threat Counter-Exploitation. New York: McGraw-Hill Osborne Media. ISBN 0071772499, ISBN 978-0071772495

http://www.hackmageddon.com/2015/08/10/july-2015-cyber-attacks-statistics/

http://www.computerworld.com/article/2559195/security0/guard-against-titan-rain-hackers.html

https://www.vanityfair.com/news/2011/03/stuxnet-201104

http://www.homelandsecuritynewswire.com/lesson-titan-rain-articulate-dangers-cyber-attack-upper-management

http://courses.cs.washington.edu/courses/csep590/05au/readings/titan.rain.htm

http://www.ynetnews.com/articles/0,7340,L-4364693,00.html

http://www.timesofisrael.com/as-cyber-war-begins-israeli-hackers-hit-back/

http://www.jpost.com/Defense/Israeli-cyber-activists-attack-anti-Israel-hackers-308921

http://blog.adl.org/international/opisrael-anonghost-anonymous-hackers-israel

http://www.forbes.com/sites/michaelpeck/2013/04/08/why-did-anonymous-have-to-attack-israel-on-holocaust-memorial-day/#760523225937

http://www.timesofisrael.com/egypts-war-of-the-streets/

https://www.icrc.org/casebook/doc/case-study/iran-victim-of-cyberwarfare.htm

http://www.businessinsider.in/The-Stuxnet-Attack-On-Irans-Nuclear-Plant-Was-Far-More-Dangerous-Than-Previously-Thought/articleshow/26113763.cms

http://arstechnica.com/tech-policy/2016/02/massive-us-planned-cyberattack-against-iran-went-well-beyond-stuxnet/

http://edition.cnn.com/2011/11/08/tech/iran-stuxnet/

http://cyberwarzone.com/

http://www.jpost.com/Blogs/Internet-Engagement/OpIsrael-Backfires-364746

http://tribune.com.pk/story/83967/36-government-websites-hacked-by-indian-cyber-army/

Stuxnet Worm Impact on Industrial

Cyber-Physical System Security - https://papers.duckdns.org/files/2011_IECON_stuxnet.pdf

http://in.pcmag.com/software/69540/news/indonesia-tops-china-as-cyber-attack-capital

http://dl.acm.org/citation.cfm?id=2818550

http://edition.cnn.com/2015/05/17/us/fbi-hacker-flight-computer-systems/index.html

http://www.usnews.com/news/articles/2015/06/05/china-suspected-in-theft-of-federal-employee-records

http://www.slate.com/articles/technology/future_tense/2015/06/opm_hack_it_s_a_catastrophe_here_s_how_the_government_

can_stop_the_next.html

https://www.wired.com/2015/06/opm-breach-security-privacy-debacle/

http://www.prweb.com/releases/2015/06/prweb12787823.htm

http://money.cnn.com/2015/07/10/technology/opm-hack-fingerprints/

http://www.federaltimes.com/story/government/omr/opm-cyber-report/2015/06/19/opm-breach-encryption/28985237/

http://www.usatoday.com/story/news/2016/02/22/opms-cybersecurity-chief-resigns-amid-continuing-pressure-congress/80766320/

http://www.informationisbeautiful.net/visualizations/worlds-biggest-data-breaches-hacks/

http://www.techinsider.io/cyberattacks-2015-12